THE HAPPY MIND

THE HAPPY MIND

*A Simple Guide
to Living a Happier Life
Starting Today*

KEVIN HORSLEY & LOUIS FOURIE

Copyright © 2017 by Kevin Horsley and Louis Fourie.

All Rights Reserved.

No part of this book may be reproduced, stored in retrieval systems, or transmitted by any means, electronic, mechanical, photocopying, recorded or otherwise without written permission from the author.

Cambria & Garamond fonts used with permission from Microsoft.

ISBN: 978-1-63161-038-7

Published by TCK Publishing

www.TCKPublishing.com

Get discounts and special deals on our best selling books at

www.tckpublishing.com/bookdeals

Cambria & Garamond fonts used with permission from Microsoft.

Disclaimer

The information and opinions contained in this book are presented in summary form only and intended to provide a broad understanding and knowledge of the subject under consideration. It should not be considered complete and should not replace formal advice by a licensed practitioner in any specific area related to the reader's personal wellness.

*"What a wonderful life I've had.
I only wish I'd realised it sooner."*

COLETTE

I devote this book to my lovely wife of thirty years, Anita, whose graceful presence made it easier for me to be happy.

Louis Fourie

~

This book is dedicated to two extraordinary people, my parents Harold and Julie, who demonstrated to me what happiness is.

Kevin Horsley

CONTENTS

How To Read This Book xi

Chapter 1 | The Search For Happiness 1

Chapter 2 | Happiness Is… 11

Chapter 3 | The Origin Of Unhappiness 26

Chapter 4 | Practical Guidelines, Thoughts, Suggestions
    & Reminders In The Interest Of Happiness 37

Chapter 5 | A Few Last Words 101

About The Authors 103

A Few Words Of Recognition 105

Other Books By The Authors 107

Get Book Discounts & Deals 109

One Last Thing 111

HOW TO READ THIS BOOK

YOU HAVE MORE THAN ONE option.

You can decide to read it - or some of it - **in an hour or two**. You can then put it away like many other books you have read in the past and probably retain about three percent of the information. That's the typical way of reading a book.

The second option is to **read it twice** – cover to cover – and then put it away. Statistically, you may then retain up to fifteen percent of the information. Not a bad option.

Alternatively, you could add it to your **daily reading**. Start your day by selecting one page, and convert its message into a personal commitment. In this way, the information will rub off on your behaviour and the principles will gradually become part of your thinking. This option is for people who are serious about their happiness.

The final option is to include **elements from the book in your monthly planning process**. This will ensure that the information converts into practical priorities in your day-to-day pattern of living. This is first prize!

We suggest that you make the most of this book by considering **all four options**. First, read it, read it again, continue reading it in a snippety way, and then assimilate the principles into your life. Convert the content into a customised happiness manual. Your happiness is important enough to do it in this way. Choose to affect the rest of your life positively.

And by the way, take notes and capture your thinking and mark what's important to you. Turn it into two books!

The principles covered in this book are for the young and the old, and for people of all cultures, any religion and both genders. Happiness is an 'any-time-in-your-life' prospect, a 'whoever-you-are' opportunity, a 'doesn't-matter-where-you-come-from' break. If you are willing to open your mind to the idea of happiness and to do what it takes, you may pleasantly surprise yourself.

The layout of the book is simple.

The **first three chapters** consist of a crisp look at what happiness is perceived to be, what it really is, and what unhappiness looks like.

In **Chapter 4**, we offer you a collection of carefully selected practical prompts to help you carry the theory of happiness into your life. This is the most important part of the book – trust the content.

And in **Chapter 5**, we offer you the gist of it all in a final few words of encouragement.

Make the most of it. Don't look for perfection, look for value. Enjoy!

CHAPTER 1

THE SEARCH FOR HAPPINESS

WHAT IS HAPPINESS? WHAT CAUSES it? How do you hold onto it? What makes it go away?

These are questions that led to many philosophical debates, over literally thousands of years. The philosophers of Greece were famous for their quest to define the pillars of 'the good life'. Faith-based movements have painstakingly crafted dogmas and prescribed behaviours in pursuit of ultimate peace and joy. Academic studies have been concentrated on finding the answer to 'the optimal life experience'. Generations of national governments have professed to craft policies in promotion of the overall wellbeing of their citizens. And many ordinary dinner table discussions, every day, are at heart a dialogue in search of a happy life.

Definitions and suggestions of what happiness is differ widely. It is a subject that lends itself to intense subjectivity. Some definitions are very specific, some open-ended. Some are heavily influenced by immediate circumstances. Some again are tainted by esoteric points of departure. Many definitions are spiritually loaded, others very pragmatic. And some guardians of these different viewpoints are quite 'unhappy' when you voice an opinion that may differ from theirs. A conversation about happiness frequently ends in stalemate. Pinning down a generally accepted definition in any non-exact field, more so for those with an emotional flavour, is never easy.

Despite different viewpoints, everyone seems to agree that it is important to be happy. In fact, we think it is fair to presume that the pursuit of happiness is our most fundamental reality.

WHAT IS YOUR DEFINITION OF HAPPINESS?

The aim of this book is not to push a specific definition of happiness. Our goal is to try and present you with valuable insights and create the private intellectual space for you to consider the subject of personal happiness, and of course to try and convince you that it is within your reach.

It consequently makes sense to start off by revisiting your personal definition of happiness. If someone asks you today to explain the ingredients of happiness, how would your explanation roughly go? What would you identify as the foundation for sustainable contentment? How would you explain it to a child – even better, to your own child? Sit back and think about it for a good few minutes. Write down the key concepts and words you would use in your first go at such a definition. Don't rush it; it's an important personal entry into the subject.

Keep this first basic explanation and key words of yours until you have finished the book. The idea is to adjust this definition when and if you gain different insights from the book, or from your own subsequent reflection on the topic. Ideally, you should conclude this journey by defining happiness along the principles you would like to apply in your own life.

Do you agree that it's not that simple to give a clear-cut definition of what happiness is? And even if you take a stab at it, you aren't too convinced that your definition is a complete one? You also probably realize it will differ from someone else's definition and you understand that the longer you ponder and work on it, the more your views may evolve?

It's a tough nut to crack, this 'science of bliss', even for those of us who aced all those other difficult exams!

Don't worry, it's common. Nobody has ever sat us down in a classroom - or even in our own living rooms as kids - and talked us through such a definition. We have been taught a million other 'how-to' formulas in many other fields. Yet no-one has ever guided us to understand the full meaning of happiness and its roots, nor taught us how to attain it, not in Western doctrines anyway. Most people from our 'clan' therefore struggle to give a conclusive definition, however bright they may be in other 'subjects'. Opinions differ widely and descriptions are often vague. Many of us actually have more questions than answers on the enquiry of what happiness is.

THE GENERAL PERCEPTION

Research shows that most people view happiness as the result of something exceptional that should happen to them. They believe happiness is **an external phenomenon that crosses your path and changes your life** for the better.

Many of the run-of-the-mill personal happiness definitions are consequently linked to a name, place, date, event, or quantity – all phenomena that may cause some form of interim pleasure, comfort, or novelty value. In other words, something that gives you an 'emotional kick' or immediate relief of some sort. People mostly tend to describe happiness in the form of 'nouns'; something you can touch, look at, show off, experience, refer to, remember, arrive at or calculate. Something you can push in a shopping trolley, someone in the passenger seat, a street address, an amount on a bank statement...

It's time to check your initial definition. Are some of these magic external influences included in your view of happiness as well? Do you also believe happiness is something 'out there' that may happen to you? Take a few seconds to circle the 'nouns' in your definition. Don't judge yourself while doing it; just quietly reflect upon your initial view.

When we take a closer look at the typical ways in which people define happiness, the 'nouns' we pick up in the descriptions all have an identical function. They act as **'if-then' assurances** - imaginary triggers underpinning a promise to uplifting experiences. **"If this or that happens, I will be happy"**, this proposition of happiness goes. People typically regard these 'nouns' as stimuli that will trigger some form of change in their personal circumstances, which should, they believe, cause a permanent modification in the way they feel about, experience, and view life. And this 'if-then' chain reaction, they presume, will culminate in a magic breakthrough called 'happiness'.

Broadly speaking, this approach to happiness leaves you convinced that happiness:

*Comes **from 'the world'** in some or other form.*

*Is in **'another time.'***

*Happens **because of 'other people.'***

A word or two on each of these popular convictions:

HAPPINESS COMES FROM 'THE WORLD'

This quest for happiness leads many people to become eternal 'treasure hunters' in the big, wide world. They **frantically seek the secret door** to happiness to be found in some or other idyllic set of circumstances. They are forever on a mission to discover their fortune of happiness - a sensation of some sort, hidden out there somewhere, waiting to be unearthed somehow.

People who believe the treasure of happiness is to be received from 'the world', usually have a considerable **fascination with wealth**. They admire the rich and famous and passionately idealise their lifestyles, even though they may witness many well-off, miserable people every day. Their thoughts calculate their potential happiness level and they are able to instantly attach currency value to it.

For them, the answer is simple: affluence holds the key to happiness. Excessive economic gravitas will do it! They are hooked by the belief that happiness grows, dollar by dollar, in linear fashion. They have settled for a simple philosophy; the more you have, the more you are. They live one long daydream of having more purchasing power. Ironically, these dreams continue even after they have attained material affluence. Once bitten by this craving, 'more' never really turns into 'enough'. Their jar of happiness has no lid.

This obsession with economic happiness often leads people to indulge in fairly irrational behaviour. Many for instance become terminal over-spenders and forever buckle under an excessive debt burden - actually impoverishing themselves in an effort to feel and look rich! Others work themselves to death or out of their family lives – subconsciously deciding to compromise their personal wellness to answer the call for more 'happiness currency'. Others again put their hope on chance or gambling, in whatever derived form, or take undue business or career risks to become wealthy sooner. Some even decide upon an all-or-nothing approach, and steal, smuggle, or defraud to quell this desire to 'have more'. There are many dishonest wealthy people, many others forever sailing close to the wind as a result of this compulsion to have more.

A final note to this 'wealth brings happiness' philosophy: Money is not the guilty party in all of this. Monetary means can in fact be valuable – and many wealthy people are happy and valued contributors to society's wellbeing. The problem arises when money is viewed and pursued as a stand-in for true happiness.

People who believe happiness comes 'from the world' often also falsely believe it **originates from status**. We may argue that it is related to the fascination with wealth, and sometimes it is. However, in essence it is about power, or an elevated position, in whatever form – whether related or unrelated to riches. It is about enjoying a standing of relative authority – albeit only in appearance or title. Some even do their utmost to marry into it, study themselves into it, campaign for it, or again, slavishly work themselves into it.

> *"While trying to find yourself in things,*
> *you may end up losing yourself in things."*
> ECKHART TOLLE

In searching for status, organisational or political pedestals come as important psychological benefits. It symbolises 'importance'. That is why status-hunters often envision an important corporate position or public title as a pivotal happiness trigger. To secure this sensation of emotional reassurance, people may even damage others' wellbeing subliminally or explicitly, when they perceive them a threat to their pursuit for professional status.

When looking further afield for a happiness trigger 'from the world', people often settle on a **demographic solution.** They will arrive at joy when they change their location, because it's not where they're living now. They are restless and are always ready to pack up and go. A different place will do it for them.

For this nomadic group of happiness chasers, the castle in the air may be a dwelling in a different neighbourhood (normally upmarket). Others are on the lookout for a view of a mountain or the sound of waves breaking in the distance, or deafening silence at night, maybe the call of a fish eagle, all for happiness to start. For some people in this frame of mind, there is often no alternative route to imaginary happiness, but to pack up and move to a different country. They believe happiness starts the moment the containers have been emptied.

A last example of happiness originating 'from the world': There are people who are on a constant mission to **improve their physical appearance**, as they are convinced that good looks and youthfulness holds the key to a happier life. They push the boundaries of visual pretension and genetic accolades - and often end up beyond the point of looking decent, some even as mobile showcases. In fact, the promise of attractiveness and beauty, in whatever form, has resulted in huge industries! Nip and tuck offerings, hair boutiques, designer clothing, trophy restaurants... you name it, are all flourishing on the obsession to 'appear' in charge, because it will spill over in happiness.

Again, there is nothing wrong with caring for yourself and harnessing your person. The problem is in the 'if-then' happiness equation that may be attached to it, in the belief that a superior projection of yourself will unlock sustained bliss and that happiness is to be found in a 'makeover'.

And so, people scrutinise 'the world', day in and day out, imagining or pursuing perceived conditions of happiness. We've touched on only a handful of examples; there are many more 'from the world' beacons.

What is your take on this view of happiness? Do you target a form of 'access' to bliss, an object that will unveil it, or an altered situation 'out there' as your guarantee to happiness? Do you believe an impulse from 'the world' holds the key to sustained contentment? Do you wait for happiness to 'arrive'?

HAPPINESS IS IN ANOTHER TIME

The second 'if-then' experience people often target for a happiness response is 'a change in time'. Many people believe happiness is wrapped up in the **passing or reversing of their present**. They are time travelling day in and day out, dreaming of another time zone in their lives – one to come, or one gone by.

This view of happiness may usually make people **spend a lot of their present in an imaginary future**. One day, they believe, happiness will descend upon them. They are 'when-this-is-over' happiness hunters. They are forever longing for a futuristic knight of happiness to gallop into their lives and liberate them from the present.

They imagine 'the happiest day of my life' without end. For them, happiness is always something to await, a future landmark, an 'as-soon-as' time zone, the spell after this. Their present is a mere stepping-stone, an exercise in day-dreaming.

Many people extend this definition of happiness even beyond their own lifetimes. Whatever the religious persuasion, tradition, or spirituality they base their view on; 'eternity' or the 'hereafter' is seen as the true door to happiness, the only time they look forward to. For those who harbour this mindset, life on earth is a mere temporary nuisance to overcome, in preparation for real happiness.

Along a similar vein, some happiness time travellers also **spend a lot of time in the past**, finding consolation in what used to be. Even more so if they gave up on their future. They never-endingly glance over their shoulder. The good old days offer them an escape from present realities and they relive parts of their lives over and over again. They are often so in love with their past that they even refer to difficult times gone by with nostalgia – anything is better than the present!

> *"The happy have whole days*
> *And those they choose.*
> *The unhappy have but hours*
> *And those they lose."*
> COLLEY CIBBER

For some of these happiness 'historians', the opposite also often occurs. They spend a lifetime trying to undo past events and decisions, because such a self-generated memory correction, they believe, will be the stimulus to happiness. If they can slice away certain recollections and bleach the past from memory, a door to a second chance, called happiness will open. They keep their present occupied with the most disempowering quest possible – trying to reset the past.

Do you desire to escape the present, as a habit, often many times a day? Do you time-travel to find happiness? Are your days consumed by dreams of 'another time'? Do you realize that tomorrow will be another 'today' when you get there? Are you aware that there is no door to your past? Do you spend a lot of time where you cannot be?

HAPPINESS HAPPENS BECAUSE OF OTHER PEOPLE

The third mirage of happiness that some gaze towards is other people. This belief is linked to three simple words when happiness is defined: she, they and he. This belief boils down to: "My happiness is in someone else's hands". Happiness has feet, hands and a voice – and enters through a door, they truly believe.

People with this mindset are inclined to perceive the seed of their happiness in what other people can do for or to them, or in what missing dimension these outsiders could carry into their lives. They therefore also tend to blame others and use them as excuses for their lack of happiness - or are envious of what they perceive others to be, to have or to withhold from them. Their happiness descriptors are referrals to someone else, the narrative of their lives a script with many actors.

At the most intimate level, many people seek happiness in or **through a life partner**. They believe that another person out there holds the key to living happily ever after. They idealise the perfect partner from an early age and enter such a relationship with amazingly lofty expectations for happiness. Paradoxically, for those who enter this relationship unhappy, this partner then often also becomes the object of their unhappiness.

When two people don't 'discover' happiness in their life partnership, one or both may **bargain on a child** to instil happiness in their lives.

So often, people place their responsibility to be happy on an innocent infant. "A baby will solve our relationship's inability to bring us happiness", they believe. They in effect transfer the responsibility of two adults to create their own happiness to a baby. Eventually this effort only creates a third unhappy person – the child.

When hiccups occur between life partners, those who believe happiness comes from others often opt for adultery in the hope that a third party will be the escape door to happiness. They naively believe that a lover or a next life partner will solve the crisis. They continue to look for happiness in an 'other half'.

Excessive reliance on friends and family also play an important role in the definition of happiness for those who have an intensified bias to link other people to their happiness. They tend to develop demanding social relations for all the wrong reasons, based on the social inclination that any family member or friend has the right to the intimate zone of their lives. They are often heavily dependent on the acceptance and recognition - even the intriguing bickering – that may result from this self-enforced sense of belonging. Ironically, they give these people access to their lives, then eventually blame them for their unhappiness.

> *"Happiness grows at our own firesides, and is not to be picked in strangers' gardens."*
> DOUGLAS JERROLD

For many people, **an employer** holds a very important key to their personal happiness. Security is crucial to most people, understandably so, and most of them see an employer as the ultimate guardian of their security – and therefore happiness. Many people are also heavily dependent on the social dynamics of the workplace and depend on this for a happiness stimulus, however dysfunctional the results often turn out to be. The place of work, for them, is much more than a source of income.

And then, people have an astonishing **expectation towards government** to guarantee a level of personal happiness. They view their government as the mythical provider of last resort and ultimate source of security and comfort. Just listen to some of those conversations around you, how 'unhappy' some people are about what their government has done to them or hasn't done for them. A government is a perfect punch bag for many unhappy people – any form of 'authority' is the ultimate crutch.

A last example - the seekers of people-focused happiness often **idealise personal icons**, constantly imagining themselves into someone else's position, whether physically, economically, socially or whatever other feature of someone 'of note' they aspire to. We frequently hear people say, "I wish I were more like him", or "If only I could be in her shoes", and "They are so lucky".

This category of happiness seekers longs to switch places with someone else, drive someone else's car, have someone else's kids, earn someone else's money...to fill a void. This tendency to idealise also leaves them **on the lookout for 'gurus'**, someone with all the magic answers, someone with the power to come and turn their lives around.

Where do you position yourself in this people-focused happiness domain? Are relationships a constructive element of your life, or are you looking out for happiness in the form of another person? How balanced is your dependence on people? Do you bargain on someone else to do for you what you should be doing for yourself?

This, in short, is the lens through which the majority of people, either explicitly or implicitly, tend to define happiness. They see it as the result of an external influence, imagining how 'something, someone, or sometime' will change their lives for the better. They are essentially outsourcing their happiness, waiting for it to happen to them from the outside.

CHAPTER 2

HAPPINESS IS...

THE FUNDAMENTAL FLAW IN SEARCHING for happiness 'out there' lies in **confusing pleasure for happiness**. This basic misperception leads to the belief that happiness is either a once-in-a-lifetime-delight, or the compound effect of many, more, or bigger 'pleasurables'.

There is, of course, a place for pleasure. In fact, pleasurable moments and uplifting experiences are the spice of life. Make sure that you fully enjoy the ones you choose. Just understand that their effect wears off. Pleasure cannot be hoarded and then called happiness.

True happiness is not a derived outcome of the swings in a 'pendulum of pleasure'. Happiness is the quality of the base on which the pendulum is mounted. It is not the reward of constant that-instead-of-this victories, but an overall rhythm in the way you live your life - a rhythm that applies in any context you find yourself, pleasurable or not. Although the 'if-then' notions of happiness are dominant and loud out there, the truth is that genuine **happiness is a 'now-and-here' skill**. It is the by-product of a specific way of living your life. It's not on the horizon, it's under your feet - not to be found 'up there', but 'down here'. It's not dessert, it's the meal!

Revisit your original beliefs about happiness again – those first thoughts you wrote down. Are your initial perceptions about happiness associated with enough 'now-and-here' ideas to your liking? How big is the shift you need to make in your definition to move your personal happiness from 'out there' to 'in here'?

> *"The happiest people seem to be those who have no particular cause for being happy except that they are so."*
>
> WILLIAM RALPH INGE

What are the mutual traits shared by happy people? In other words, if happiness is the offshoot of a pattern of conduct and not simply an assortment of 'highs', what are the underlying features to the pattern?

All our research, interactions and observations, have led us to conclude that happy people share nine common qualities:

1. They **think in a different way**
2. They **assume full accountability** for their circumstances
3. They **enjoy simple things** more
4. They **own up to their future**
5. They are **passionately engaged** in what they do for a living
6. They invest in their **overall wellness**
7. They have **constructive relationships**
8. They harness an **optimistic world view**
9. They accept that happiness is a **day-to-day effort**

You may get the 'chicken and egg' feeling when you look at the list. Is this what happy people do, you may ask, or is this what people do to be happy? The truth is that it's a fair portion of both. Applying these principles in your life feeds happiness, but they also come easier for people who commit to their own happiness. It doesn't really matter which comes first; what does matter is that these principles are embedded in the lives of people who are happy with who they are and with the lives they have chosen to live.

Let's pause for a moment and briefly reflect upon each of these happiness traits.

1. HAPPY PEOPLE THINK IN A DIFFERENT WAY

Happy people **view life through a productive window**. The general way in which they give meaning to every-day information and events is not tarnished by fantasies of personal threats or portrayals of what is amiss. They empower themselves with an enabling perspective on matters instead of settling for the 'downside'. They get out of the way of true answers and support lasting solutions, even though it may not be 'their' answer or solution.

The ancestor of every action in your life is a thought process. **How we think is how our lives work out**. Our reality over time mirrors the way in which we choose to make sense of life. We structure our lives in our heads.

Happy people often appear to be fortunate. However, when you examine the pattern according to which they decode life, you realise their good fortune starts in their minds. They live more harmonious lives because they don't think in contradictory or conflicting patterns. The lens through which they define life isn't scratched. They don't burden their minds with a hunger for superiority, but invite, allow and comprehend any information, accommodate more opinions, and consider alternative suggestions. They aren't 'at war' with life or set in their own ideas of 'how things should work'.

> *"Guard over your thinking, for it becomes actions.*
> *Your actions slowly turn into habits.*
> *Over time, your habits shape your character.*
> *And in the end, your character becomes your destiny.*
> *If you want to change your destiny,*
> *change your thinking."*
>
> ANON

The way in which we consider and work with information in our minds influences both the visible and invisible quality of our energy. The energy we carry originates in our heads. Happy people are energy-rich. They subject their anxieties to the authority of reason, oppose them through a spirit of compromise, and diminish them by living in peace. It allows them ease of progress in every endeavor, and they naturally do what should be done without the energy erosion accompanied by inner resistance and panic. They have an ability to accept objective solutions, as their assumptions are prejudice-lite.

Happy people are for **solutions instead of being against problems**. They carry a still power of abundance, because they don't interpret life as a place of scarcity. Their welcoming disposition towards life affords them a remarkable sense of freedom and inner peace.

How productive is the nature of attention you give to life? Does your appraisal of the world energize or drain you (and others)? How many 'enemies' do you visualize 'out there', while they may actually be friends in the waiting? Are you open to new information and learning, or are your subjective positions blocking your growth? How dramatic is the movie playing out in your head?

2. HAPPY PEOPLE ASSUME FULL ACCOUNTABILITY FOR THEIR CIRCUMSTANCES

Happy people don't live in a protective bubble – they share the 'winters and summers' of life with all other mortals. They live under the same circumstances as less happy people - but **choose to behave differently towards the ups and downs they are exposed to**.

Happy people actively take charge of their circumstances. They refuse to be imprisoned by what happens to or around them. It seems much easier for them to counter the negative effects of unfriendly conditions, while they display the habit of making the most of favorable circumstances. All this simply because of an orientation towards life. **They don't rent their lives, they own them**, under all circumstances. And their ownership extends to the cause, effect, and solution of an affair.

Research shows that circumstances can indeed play a role in a person's overall happiness level, but that circumstantial adjustments are seriously overrated in terms of their impact on our long-term happiness. True, relief from extreme financial hardship, relationship problems, physical pain or environmental discomfort could have a notable effect on a person's absolute level of happiness. But various studies have concluded that non-extreme, every-day situations don't account for more than about ten percent of the variations in people's happiness levels.

Our circumstances will always vary and always introduce unexpected moments. But if we really want to, **we can easily manage most circumstances**. Happy people believe this, and show they do by taking charge of the part they can control or utilize.

Happy and unhappy people ask different questions when an undesirable thing happens to them. Happy people ask, "What am I going to do about this?" and "How am I going to prevent this from happening again?" Unhappy people ask, "Why does this always happen to me?" or "Who is to blame for this?" In essence, happy people are willing to employ the power of choice and ownership while unhappy people opt for a sense of victimisation. Happy people work with life as it is, not as they wished it were.

All in all, our circumstances don't determine the reality of our life experience – our attitude towards them does. If you have cynical, pacifying, or inhibiting thoughts about your circumstances, your reality will be negative. It has been said that the only difference between a weed and a flower is a judgement. The same life is constantly a flower for some and a weed for others – because of the attitude towards it.

Attitude is a mental orientation. It can support or obstruct you. Every thought about your circumstances you consciously confirm to be true, will multiply. Such a thought becomes a belief. The story of your life portrays these beliefs, as they shape new consequences. When you change your pattern of attachment to circumstances, you gradually change this mental construction, and you lay a new foundation of how you manage and shape your conditions. It's a choice that offers freedom, but also a choice that needs to be backed energetically. Circumstances may originate externally – the extent of their effect on us is an internal affair.

How well do you manage circumstances and changes in your context? Do they overwhelm you time and again, or do you choose to manage them actively? Do you make things bigger than they are? Are you a victim, or are you an owner of the conditions surrounding your life?

3. HAPPY PEOPLE ENJOY SIMPLE THINGS MORE

Happy people pay attention to life in a particular way, interacting with it through all their senses.

They see more in a flower, still pause to smell it. They embrace humid sunsets as well as windy, rainy days. Tasting is still an important part of eating for them. They still have the capacity to ask a child an honest question – and hear the answer.

Their array of small, practical joys is seemingly endless. They instinctively embrace the enormity of the gift of life by **pausing at all the tiny wonders**, every day.

If you don't make time and create stillness to consciously observe and experience these wonders of life, your life experience becomes shallow and you tend to be vulnerable to every threat, however superficial or imaginary. You run on empty, all the time. If you don't stop and frequently acknowledge all the petite yet superior dimensions of life, and make time to experience them, your soul shrinks and your 'needs' will dominate your life story.

Life offers its fullness to us every day, yet so many of us opt for emotional starvation. Happy people nurture the habit of fully experiencing the content of their every-day reality and **inquisitively finding the nuggets of positive influence** in that reality.

This enjoyment of the bits of beauty and awareness of the small treasures fuels a special form of gratitude – deep, consistent appreciation. Gratitude is probably the single most telling characteristic of happiness, as the ability to unconditionally appreciate is the ultimate counter-force to those monstrous human self-destructors – anger, arrogance, desire, indifference, regret, resentment and guilt.

Gratitude is the most unselfish form of love. It represents a mindfulness beyond guilt or indebtedness. It presents gifts of serenity not even sought for, unveils grace in moments of pain. It gently enforces perspective and humility. No form of fear can hold its own when confronted with true gratitude. It empowers, beyond imagination. It is the parent of virtues.

Happy people are grateful people. They need less because they experience abundance. If you decide to forget everything you have read in this book, remember this sentence: **APPRECIATE**

compulsively, learn to derive more joy from simple delights - and you will be in touch with real happiness, every moment.

Are you aware of the treasures around you and in your life? Do you make time to ponder at and enjoy life's generous handouts? How relevant are your needs? Do you actively practise gratitude?

4. HAPPY PEOPLE OWN UP TO THEIR FUTURE

Happy people take ownership of every situation they are in; they take charge of their future. They accept that at the start of every year, every month, every week, every day - their lives are a clean track of snow and that it is for them to decide how and where they will leave their footprints. They don't opt for helplessness, and don't settle for the belief that one's future is 'pre-determined'. They are deeply aware of the fact that **life is not a rehearsal**, so they choose carefully, actively, and continuously when they allocate their effort.

Happy people refuse to live by chance. They take focused, decisive, and constructive steps to realize their plans. They accept that these steps don't always guarantee or lead to the perfect outcome, but they nonetheless hold themselves to a philosophy that 'decisiveness guarantees progress'.

Again, remember that happy people don't spend their days nestled between lilywhite cotton sheets. They live real lives under real circumstances. But they suffer much less, because they **prevent many things from going wrong** through strong, pre-contemplated decision-making. They adjust to new conditions, and when necessary, even create them. They change what they can. They influence outcome. They are open-minded yet strong-willed in their approach to their future.

How do they do it? First, they **make planning a priority activity** in their lives. They devote ample time to it, as a scheduled routine, and build supportive processes around it. Their agenda consists of four main headings, in a specific order: Personal wellness, Family sturdiness, Professional progress and Wider community joy. It covers all the bases of their lives, and reflects the pattern of a constructive life plan – starting with oneself.

Secondly, they are very clear about the nature of their journey. **They know what their purpose in life is, and have defined their**

inspirations and aspirations. They live according to a chosen set of principles, which buffers them from being distracted by surface solutions, quick fixes, or other people's lives. They are even willing to revisit their values, beliefs, and assumptions about life if the facts upon which they based them have changed, or their insights have matured.

Thirdly, happy people **set themselves constructive objectives**, personally and professionally. They are clear about their goals, which enable them to set priorities. Their days, consequently, are characterized by simplicity and directional savvy, because they know what to keep in focus, which tasks are secondary, and what to let go. Their diaries mirror their priorities.

A life marked by ownership, planning, and priorities enjoys a huge happiness advantage. It gives personal meaning to the activity of living. It allows you the joy of completion and accomplishment. It limits waste.

Do you make dynamic decisions about the quality of your future - or are you waiting for the future to 'happen to you'? Are you on course in all facets of your life? Do you set aside the time to plan? Are you a responsible guardian of your own life?

> *"There are two ways to live your life.
> One is as though nothing is a miracle.
> The other is as if everything is a miracle."*
> ALBERT EINSTEIN

5. HAPPY PEOPLE ARE PASSIONATELY ENGAGED IN WHAT THEY DO FOR A LIVING

Happy people fully embrace what they choose to do. When they are on holiday, they are fully there. When they read, they take in every ounce of information. When they practise their faith, they afford their spirit optimal growth. When they choose to retire, they fill the freedom with joyful content. When they listen to music, they hear every nuance.

Full engagement is a practice of passion. It is rooted in **an excitement to be alive**.

Happy people draw no obvious distinction between their work and their play; they always appear to be doing both. They enjoy their lives, even when they are busy earning their living; they don't spend their working lives 'slaving away' at a product they cannot really represent. They are clear about their own path of value creation instead of chasing after the dreams of others or imitating someone else's skills.

Happy people respect and **play according to their own strengths** and allow aspirations associated to those strengths to shape their potential. Obviously, it takes courage to do what you love for a living – or to reshape what you do until it inspires you. You need a strong will to afford your career the magic combination of heart, skill and intent, instead of simply 'doing a job' or 'turning up' every day. You need a lot of self-motivation to professionally practise what you believe in.

> *"Most people are other people.*
> *Their thoughts are someone else's opinions,*
> *their lives a mimicry,*
> *their passions a quotation."*
> OSCAR WILDE

Happy people show this courage. They fit their careers around a personal quest – **a journey that captures their attention and intelligence**. They allow their intrinsic field of fascination to become a real-life experience. And this engagement in their 'task of will' leaves them with an abundance of energy, which empowers them to become great at what they do and allows them an 'unfair' competitive edge. Their souls are on fire when they work!

Do you make the most of every engagement you decide upon? Are you energized by the challenges of your professional field? Have you given yourself permission to be in love with life? Do you show the courage to make changes to the content of your job until it fits your sweet spot? Are you on a professional mission with personal significance? Are you wholly engaged?

6. HAPPY PEOPLE INVEST IN THEIR OVERALL WELLNESS

Happy people regard themselves. They treasure the gift of life and accept responsibility for their own wellbeing.

Happy people **care for their physical health**. Although numerous studies have shown that people with disabilities and chronic illnesses can also be content and at peace as well, your body remains your central control system. It's the head office of your life! It's so much better to assist it to assist you. Without energy or with pain and discomfort, life is just 'less easy'.

Happy people normally stick to a simple health regime. First, they are sufficiently conscious about what they consume. They hold themselves to a balanced diet rich in natural immune boosters, they drink at least seven glasses of water a day, they limit the intake of animal fat, refined carbohydrates, and simple sugars, and they avoid smoking and the use of other unnatural substances. They secondly get ample exercise. They understand that exercise produces endorphins that sooth the brain and energise the body. That fitness strengthens our immune system, protects our cardio-vascular network, and keeps our frame intact. Thirdly, they sleep well. They understand the importance of recovery in a world hostile to rest – and in which many modern ailments can be linked to reduced immunity flowing from our habit of 'under-sleeping'.

Happy people also **take care of their spiritual growth**. They afford themselves a purpose to their lives - a quest with personal meaning through which they make a real difference, every day. They nurture their souls by surrounding themselves with constructive people and a positive personal environment. They choose simplicity and avoid boredom. They embrace lightheartedness.

Happy people make time to silently reflect on the good things in life. They harness the peace encapsulated in inner completeness, whether practicing it through meditation, prayer, or traditional rituals, regularly allowing their 'minds to come home'.

A happy spirit normally contributes to a happy body.

Happy people also ensure that they continue to **invest in their intellectual capacity**. They respect the fact that our cognitive abilities can forever be sculpted by intent. They realize that our brain is constantly changing - and changeable - and that strengthening it takes mindful effort. Our brain is an integral part of our physicality, which means 'what's good for your body is good for your brain', and of course 'what is good for the brain also serves the body'.

Happy people nurture their intelligence by retaining their curiosity and inviting new information and unfamiliar learning into their lives. They often teach, create, converse or write – which compels them to challenge their synaptic connections through the process of reflective fermentation of existing information.

Finally, happy people **attend to their personal financial wellbeing**. They hold themselves to simple principles and

time-tested realities: They spend less than they earn, and so limit their lifetime cost of debt. They aren't obsessed with symbols of wealth, and so waste less money. They don't compete with the neighbors, which makes it easier for them to save. They focus on their primary competency, which allows them to earn a good income. They invest in the happiness of their family, and so shape secure, 'inexpensive' children. They have realistic expectations when they invest their savings, and therefore earn better long-term returns on their assets. They plan their retirement, and therefore achieve financial independence. They don't make enemies, which keeps them out of expensive tiffs. And they are not victims of crises, because they plan well and so prevent many setbacks.

Do you actively invest in your wellness? Do you consciously nurture all the components and dimensions of your life? Do you neglect yourself because you suffer of a false moral dilemma, believing that caring for yourself is 'selfish'? Are you serious enough about preserving the multi-facetted life you have been blessed with? Do you believe prevention is better than cure?

7. HAPPY PEOPLE HAVE CONSTRUCTIVE RELATIONSHIPS

To be happy, it is important to get along with people. A life of social harmony makes the travel much lighter.

Before engaging others and spending their effort on strangers, happy people are firstly aware of the **importance of being their own best friends**. They are fine with being in their own company, and aren't in permanent escape mode when alone. Alone doesn't mean 'lonely' for happy people. Their most important relationship – with themselves – is intact, guilt-free, undemanding, and a calming experience.

Because this primary relationship is intact, happy people also have sound relationships with those around them. We have not been made to live in isolation. Virtually all happiness research of significance underscores the importance of positive relationships with family, friends and members of the communities we belong to. We remain in essence an 'ultra-social' tribe and our associations with others address our deep-seated need to collaborate, to be accepted and to share the spoils.

Happy people are great relationship gatekeepers. They are good friends, but only to good friends. They don't measure the quality of their relationship experience by the number of people in their lives. They **carefully select their relationships**. They don't associate with destructive or self-centered people. They walk away from negative attitudes and toxic mentalities. They don't fall prey to abusive associations. Happy people don't see this choice of relative exclusivity as being selfish, but as self-preserving.

> *"There's one sad truth in life I've found*
> *While journeying east and west –*
> *The only folks we really wound*
> *Are those we love the best.*
> *We flatter those we scarcely know,*
> *We please the fleeting guest,*
> *And deal full many a thoughtless blow*
> *To those who love us best."*
>
> ELLA WHEELER WILCOX

Positive relationships are like a campfire – you have to feed them to prevent them from burning out. To lighten each other's burdens and share each other's joy is energy intensive. **'Less' is therefore more**. To invite too many people into our lives is like trying to spread a thousand loaves with a single bowl of butter. Apparently, we are wired to maintain roughly five to seven relationships well; anything more causes quality leakage, exhaustion, and unnatural behavior. It normally leads to all your relationships becoming superficial and unsustainable. Solid relationships aren't 'crowd-compliant'.

This doesn't mean that happy people don't know many people and have more than a handful of acquaintances; it just comes down to the fact that they realize you can't intimately invest in more relationships than you are humanly capable of sustaining. And they are conscious that, after relating well to themselves, **the first in line for quality attention are those people who share a roof with them, the members of their household**. When Mother Teresa received the Nobel Prize she was asked: "What can we do to promote world peace?" She replied, "Go home and love your families." A great source of unhappiness is people's focus on fringe relationships and the neglect of their most intimate ones.

How would you rate the quality of your relationships? Are you peaceful in your own company? Do you leave people better off? Do your relationships overwhelm or strengthen you? Are the members of your immediate family a priority in word and deed?

8. HAPPY PEOPLE HARNESS AN OPTIMISTIC WORLD VIEW

Happy people are positive people. They view and approach life through a filter of realism, yet retain an **infectious enthusiasm about life in general**. They choose to live 'less serious' lives.

Practical optimism is an action-orientated mindset, not a 'feel good', or ignoring the brutal facts of life. It's founded on the 'productive window' on life discussed earlier, in other words a solution-seeking attitude instead of being paralyzed by fear. It's about being hopeful because you are willing to do what it takes to improve the outcome; about eagerly learning lessons, being involved in refining and implementing improvements to your practice of living. Real positivism is about solving and preventing problems, not laughing them off or naively looking away when they occur. It's a capacity to view failure as temporary, limited, and a part of life – and then moving on to a solution.

A positive mindset demands that you don't hoard baggage. Happy people put the past behind them. They forgive easier. They don't waste energy on carrying grudges and playing judge. They are not energized through revenge. This attitude in some sense echoes Shakespeare's words, "I would rather have a fool make me merry, than experience make me sad". They have resolved that being glum is the most unproductive way of spending their present.

Happy people **see the funny side to life**. They can chuckle at life and laugh at themselves – and they do it often. They enjoy humor for what it is – a very efficient shock absorber to life's turbulent moments, exposing all those ironic gaps between beliefs and reality, between trivial and important. They have a resilient spirit. When they smile, they smile with their eyes. They carry lightness.

Does your view of life make things easier or more difficult for you? Do your opinions energize and inspire, or do they dent the spirit of those exposed to you? Do you solve problems or do you sulk about them? Do you laugh enough? Do you move on or do you get stuck?

9. HAPPY PEOPLE ACCEPT THAT HAPPINESS IS A DAY-TO-DAY EFFORT

Now for the sobering part – leaving the crucial message for last. **Happiness is work!**

Being miserable is infinitely easier than being happy. Because many of life's moments carry the capacity to turn on us – if we allow them to. We are practically surrounded by unhappiness traps – inside ourselves and in our circumstances. So, if we don't attune our minds and actions to counter these pitfalls every day, we will surely fall victim to many of them. Our complex society and apprehensive nature invite us to self-destruct and make life very personal.

Happiness is therefore a thing to be practiced, "like a violin", someone once said. Happy people start by giving themselves the go-ahead to be happy. Then they work at it, every day, starting with a clean slate, to keep this permission alive. They approach it with serious intent, yet conquer it one step at a time.

If you are not committed to this consistent effort, happiness will be difficult to sustain. **Nothing worthwhile ever comes easy or quick**. It's no different from your life in other spheres. Your thirst isn't quenched forever when you drink a glass of water; your bills aren't paid forever if you don't return to work tomorrow; you don't stay fit if you don't exercise again and again. And so, you won't be afforded unconditional happiness, without consistently doing what needs to be done to keep your life aligned to the disciplines of bliss.

Alexandre Dumas once said, "Happiness is like those palaces in fairy tales whose gates are guarded by dragons; we must fight to conquer it". Happy people take on this challenge with renewed enthusiasm, every day. This is the reason for the second part of this book – to help you create a framework within which this 'work' makes sense.

Always remember what they say about overnight success – it's normally **years in the making**. Happiness is a classic example of such an 'overnight success'!

And that's it. These are the nine principles that direct and characterize the lives of truly happy people. It sounds simple and most of it should actually come across as general knowledge, but you will be surprised how many people regard them as too simple. They keep on searching for the secret.

We know each of these nine points justifies a book on its own. We simply want to sensitize you to each and invite you to wrap them around your own life. Recall them often as reminders to direct your personal happiness journey. Test yourself daily against these principles. Build your own strategy and routines around them. Treasure and upgrade those already in place in your life. You could even consider to, in time, read a good book on each of these principles.

> *"Action may not always bring happiness; but there is no happiness without action."*
> BENJAMIN DISRAELI

CHAPTER 3

THE ORIGIN OF UNHAPPINESS

WHY RETURN TO UNHAPPINESS, YOU may be asking, when we are just about getting the drift of what happiness is? The answer is simple: happiness is the type of subject you understand even better when you ponder its foe for a moment. By spending a few moments on the opposite end of the happiness scale, you also have an opportunity to subconsciously audit your own proneness to unhappiness.

THE INGREDIENTS OF UNHAPPINESS

Unhappiness is not about having more downs than ups. It is about going through life forever desiring something else. It's a **state of lasting discontentment**, for different reasons at different times. When you analyze the phenomenon of 'inner poverty', it comes down to the inverse of the happiness principles we covered in the previous chapter.

The degree of unhappiness may vary from person to person, and the prevalence of some of the principles more dominant than others. We are also deeply aware of the fact that there might be serious medical or psychiatric grounds for some people's bleak life experience. Barring these conditions, the root cause of a life of discontentment is to be found in a combination of the following dispositions:

- A destructive thinking pattern

Unhappy people entertain a thinking pattern that turns everyday conditions into a dramatic mental script, a storyline in which victims, villains, and rescuers dominate the 'movie'. They crudely classify situations as rewards and threats, categorize people as friends or foes, and value outcome as a personal loss or gain.

Essentially they spend their lives in survival mode, exhausting themselves by framing life as a win-lose experience, defending themselves against illusionary enemies, and responding in some forceful way to these fears.

These degrees of inner agony leave them susceptible to superficial solutions, to control by 'liberators' and to expensive remedies. A hostile mind shapes a hostile personal world.

- Being a passive victim of circumstances

Unhappy people freeze or panic in the face of challenging conditions. They easily succumb to the blows of life – opting for bitterness instead of betterness. They are on a never-ending mission to delegate accountability.

Finding culprits gives them more satisfaction than finding solutions. What happens around them often ends up being a very personal, explosive affair. They frequently surrender to illusionary harm, often spending time in the alleys of history. They are masterful at explaining the nature of their complaints.

- Being generally dissatisfied

Unhappy people ooze a spirit of discontentment – and therefore tend to stumble from conflict to quarrel. Something is always 'blowing up or burning down', or the feeling that something is about to.

> "The brick walls are not there to keep us out.
> The brick walls are there to give us a chance to show how badly we want something.
> The brick walls are there to stop the people who don't want it badly enough."
>
> RANDY PAUSCH

It is difficult for them to enjoy simple things. In fact, they find many of the generous gifts of life irritating because of its lack of substance, or aren't even aware of them. They are caught in a wedge between what they have and what they argue they should have. Their preoccupations centre around 'what's lacking'.

They find it difficult to love, even more so when you add the word 'unconditional' to love. They argue that, to unreservedly accept and care for life and its variety of role players, is an unfair expectation. Gratitude is at best an occasional moment of good religious manners to them. They are often glad when a day ends.

- Bargaining on chance – then forever blaming someone or something

Unhappy people leave their future to happen to them. Their tomorrows are in someone else's hands. They never find time to plan. They consequently learn to hide behind a mentality of confessions, resentment, and guilt trips.

They are always ready to identify the perpetrator. And they spend endless hours in illusionary – sometimes even real - court cases, finding someone else at fault, reaping their limited moments of meaning at someone else's expense, and bringing someone to book.

All of this turmoil is because the definition of their lives and the quality of their future have been 'outsourced' – and are therefore normally hijacked by 'offenders'.

- Living a disconnect

Unhappy people are masterful 'dislikers'. They always want something else. When they are at work, they want to retire. When they are retired, they want to work.

Professionally, they are 'doing someone else's job' for a living. Their passion has remained a theoretical reference. Their career and workplace is essentially a source of misery. Their hearts aren't there and their best energy spent on something else.

This lack of engagement inhibits their contribution and often leaves them economically deprived, whatever their native level of talent. They have settled for professional detachment and a soulless work experience. And it starts with the fact that they aren't too excited about life itself.

- Abusing or disregarding themselves

Unhappy people aren't well – and normally don't look, sound, or feel well. They neglect their health, allow their spirit to run dry and become intellectually lazy.

It shows in the second half of their lives, when youthfulness doesn't coat the damage anymore. Their finances are ever so often a mess. Their scars of discontentment exhibit themselves in their appearance, sentiment, and behavior.

They blame the disrepair on a 'hostile environment'. But the vandalizing actually started long ago, sadly often by indifferent parents, and then continued as a personal style. They passively oversee an unnecessary erosion of their lives – essentially opting for treatment instead of avoidance.

- Being isolated from – or overwhelmed by people

Unhappy people are often insecure. This may mean that they hide from people or on the other side of the social scale, that they invite every stranger into their lives as 'friends'. Their relationships are marked by unnatural constraints and obligations, constituting a social pendulum swinging between dependence and rejection.

Their associations are regularly burdened by control and forceful interactions – normally because of being exposed to such relationship models early in their lives. They usually allow a crooked ranking of relationships, not befriending themselves, attending to those in their own households first, before allowing outsiders into their lives.

- Being cynical and negative

Unhappy people can spread contagious pessimism and erode the spirit of those around them. They are masters at describing a problem or designing dooms-day scenarios and at dressing up hopelessness.

Their conversations are built around personal criticism and general objections. It's as if they are happy when they can be unhappy! They expect the worst from life; worrying and grieving offer them a strange sense of satisfaction. They view their setbacks as permanent, pervasive, and personal.

They extract energy from trying to prove that life is a dark and dangerous place. They are often depressed.

> *"Failure is seldom a single, cataclysmic event.*
> *Failure is a few errors in judgement,*
> *repeated every day."*
>
> JIM ROHN

- Passively accepting unhappiness as their fate

They don't regard happiness as a verb and a concept that they can actually do something about. They are simply the 'unlucky' ones, not destined for inner harmony and outer advancement.

They focus on what they don't want or have in life, instead of concentrating on what they want and can do about it. They spend their days in defensive mode. They depend on a flawed formula for happiness.

How depressing it is to just review this selection of unhappiness traits! It's one long description of severe inner turmoil. Skim the list once more and recall a person you know who shows some of these destructive symptoms. And can you recall a person who does not display any of these traits? Do you agree that the first person is someone you will not exactly describe as happy, while the second one may very well strike you as happy?

And what about you? Do you perhaps **recognise some of these 'habits of unhappiness' in your own life?** If you do, do you realize it's probably a subconscious decision to hold onto them? You are free to blame your parents for them, but at a certain point in your life, looking over your shoulder for the reasons of some of these traits in your life just doesn't cut it anymore.

How willing are you to admit it or do something about it? Do you realize how difficult you make it for yourself and people around you if you accommodate these behaviors?

Just a reminder again, as is the case with happiness, unhappiness is not necessarily an absolute state. Some people are 'less unhappy' than others. The point remains that 'less unhappy' still doesn't mean happy. And the remedy is simple – starting to consciously chip away at it, every day, stopping yourself when you digress, saying no when you see it coming.

Why are some of us unhappy?

This brings us to the million-dollar question. What makes people choose to be unhappy? Ongoing despondency and despair can clearly not be a rational choice. Why then do some opt for the traits described above – or why do they fall prey to them?

A fundamental source of unhappiness relates to an **inability to control primitive instincts**. Sociologists make no bones about the fact that intellectually and emotionally, we might have significantly outgrown our Stone-age neurology, but that when it really matters, our instincts still merrily dictate how we conduct our lives. We may appear and sound civilised, they argue, but when the chips are down, we act surprisingly primitively. Our 'old brain' is well and alive.

The essence of this theorem originates from the standpoint that, while we are able to solve many of our present-day, self-made complexities, we still shudder when confronted with two **ancient life-threatening notions; rejection and scarcity**. In other words, the fears of not 'having enough' and not 'being enough'; and so being excluded from the primary circle of life.

The scientific argument goes that these fears are the result of a neural network still at work in our brain, which once helped us to survive as a species. As you may know, they call it our 'fight or flight' instincts. Simply put, these instincts cause our 'rational, present-day' brain to be much more of an obedient servant than we would have liked it to be. We default to survival mode in a blink, notwithstanding all the proof that we don't have to be in survival mode any longer. Nobody has ever unplugged our 'primitive' brain to relieve us of all its outdated messages!

TEN UNHAPPINESS TRAPS

1. Look for the hurt in things

2. Find the enemy in others

3. A poor-me attitude

4. A craving for validation

5. Compare and compete

6. Upsizing life's imperfections

7. Dramatizing your past

8. Conditional love

9. Trying to change someone

10. Fear-casting the future

(Try to articulate the opposites of these behaviors for your own use)

Failing to keep this basic biological circuitry of fear under control, we believe, is one of the greatest enemies of happiness. These days, **what is good for survival is often bad for happiness**. To allay one's primitive fears in a world that is much more abstract and no longer 'jungle-friendly' - and in which survival has become a gentle and mostly symbolic affair - is often disastrous and counter-productive. Our primary stress hormones don't serve us very well any longer.

Look around you; listen carefully. Do you see and hear the 'symbolic' efforts of people to quell their fears of 'rejection' and 'scarcity'? Do you recognize how many people live life virtually unconsciously, allowing these archaic forces to dictate to them how they should fill their days? Their fear of failure leads their thought process and plays a role in many of their important decisions.

Do you understand why people will buy what they cannot afford? Do you realize it is 'to be accepted' – or otherwise to temporarily smooth the deep-seated fear of 'relative scarcity'? There are so many examples of where these fears manifest themselves daily. People will have undesirable relationships or even suffer abuse, just to feel 'less rejected'. They will lose their reputation in an effort to get hold of more wealth – either to feel more secure or at least to create the image of being resource-rich, and so try to ensure acceptance. Some will even lose their health in pursuit of more wealth. People will consume what their bodies cannot really process, symbolically trying to 'stamp abundance' on their lives.

All these and many other modern ways of addressing ancient fears seriously affect people's personal happiness, because the mismatch causes immense financial, social, and psychological strains.

This ongoing, impulsive reaction to these ingrained fears of ruin has nothing to do with a lack of intelligence. It simply happens, irrespective of all the rational reasons why it shouldn't. And there is an immense urgency to it. It enforces a short-term orientation and knee-jerk responses - and the 'quick fix' industries flourish on the urge. They know very well that the therapy effect of immediate satisfaction temporarily alleviates both these calls of nature, and that people don't 'calculate' when they buy when in impulsive mode.

> *"The only thing we have to fear is fear itself."*
> FRANKLIN D. ROOSEVELT

Responsible long-term decisions will always struggle to hold up to short-term spurts of gratification. People's quest to feel 'less rejected' or 'more affluent' ever so often limits good sense.

All of us, unfortunately, carry this genetic backwardness with us, some of us just manage it better – and are therefore happier. In other words, some of us are better equipped to fear less, or have consciously steered ourselves away from these alerts of the ego. Happy people use their 'clever' brain to limit the irrelevant messages of their primeval brain. Less happy people tend to be more victimized by their archaic fear-centre – a facility not understanding or being equipped to care about one's happiness.

The practical side-effects of these neurological fears **can be radically pronounced because of traumatic childhood experiences**. In turn, they can be much more under control because of a sound upbringing. Children, who haven't experienced security, acceptance, peace, and love during early caregiving, especially during the first six years of their lives, might experience more pronounced fear as adults. If you haven't been accepted unconditionally as a child or if you have been exposed to systemic insecurity in whatever form, it might affect your inherent level of security as an adult.

The parenting we receive is therefore potentially one of the most profound exogenous differentiators in our happiness outcome when we reach adulthood. The security instilled because of good parenting acts as an ingrained buffer against outdated genetic anxieties – and therefore against underlying unhappiness. Many unhappy people had unhappy upbringings; they are more prone to fear and more inclined to display instinctive behavior, leaving them vulnerable.

The subject of upbringing justifies a book on its own – and many wonderful ones have been written over centuries, explaining the profound impact of parenting on a person's happiness. Read some of them – especially if you plan to be a parent or are busy raising a child.

Now the question begs - do the previous few pages imply that we are victims of our genetic blueprint and neurological legacy?

Well, it's for you to decide. Personally, we don't believe you need to be a victim, despite the fact that we sensitized you to these influences. In our daily work with people, we have seen remarkable shifts in people's happiness, because they wanted to and backed this decision of will with a strategy.

Be careful not to use some sort of genetic excuse as a cop-out. Sure, you can opt for the classic 'This-is-the-way-I-am' excuse or 'They say there is nothing you can do about it'. If you program your mind with the conclusion, 'I'm a victim of my parents,' or 'My fears are based on reality', you have to accept the consequences you create. Unfortunately, such capitulation will only contribute to an increase in your unhappiness.

We are a peculiar species for one outstanding reason – **we are equipped with a sophisticated decision-making ability**. We have a mind that can make higher order choices and override instinctive stimuli. The 'clever' part of the human brain, called the neocortex, holds our cognitive abilities, spiritual intelligence, emotional competence, free will and many other uniquely wonderful capabilities. If you want it to be, it can be the master of your 'fight or flight' brain.

Many people go through life unhappy, passively allowing themselves to be bamboozled by the remnants of their genetic blueprint and the outdated messages of their primitive brain. They are intellectually equipped and formula-driven in their approach to their professional success – the legacy of thousands of hours of formal education. Yet they shun their **discretionary ability to make decisions about their happiness**, and refuse to put in the hours to upgrade their capacity to be happy.

The absence of willpower and self-discipline is hard to explain. It remains difficult to clarify why people with the intellectual resources won't decisively do something about their happiness, why they elect to be victims and why they avoid the extraordinary magic of choice. The reasons given for this self-inflicted passivity or 'learned helplessness' are vague. Objectively speaking, the excuses are unconvincing as well. Hopefully, it is obvious that you should never expect sympathy from the world if you have access to all the inherent equipment for a better life, but choose to be a passive casualty.

To summarize, willpower is like an emotional muscle – a direct outflow of the use of your decision-making capacity. The more decisions you make to proactively manage your life towards more happiness and not simply react defensively or leave it to chance, the more willpower you will develop. All muscles work like that. The stronger your willpower becomes, the less you will be inclined to become a victim of genes, outdated fears, destructive habits, or irrelevant activities.

Choice is the father of freedom, as following through with action is the mother of permanent progress.

CHAPTER 4

PRACTICAL GUIDELINES, THOUGHTS, SUGGESTIONS AND REMINDERS IN THE INTEREST OF HAPPINESS

LET'S QUICKLY RECAP.

A happy life is a prolonged experience of meaning and fulfillment, a long-lasting enduring enjoyment of life, not the arrival of a mystical moment or a string of joyful events. It is the result of taking charge of every part of your day, of every day of your life, and so of your destiny. It is living from the inside out. And it has a lot to do with taking ownership of your own mind. Happiness is profound yet simple. It is an extraordinary experience – **being in harmony with the life you live, and with life itself.**

Happy people don't have special circumstances. Neither do they bargain on external windfalls. They are their own people, not exhausted competitors in someone else's race. They differ in that they select to do things differently, **think differently, and choose differently** – whatever their circumstances. They de-complicate life by the way they respond to it; and apply a mindset that positively influences every dimension of their lives.

Happiness is not 'one big thing'. It's not a single-answer solution or an instant turnaround. It doesn't arrive with fanfare. It's much less of a silky experience than people realize. It cannot be bestowed upon you. It's not a moment of glory. It's **enjoying the process as much as the outcome** and seeing life as a privilege, not a pressure cooker. Seeking happiness as a 'big moment' is in fact the antithesis of happiness. To build your happiness on things you can lose again leaves you forever vulnerable.

Happiness is the by-product of a million small things - whether actions, thoughts, or choices – habitually repeated, an integrated way of living, adding up to a lifetime experience of inner wellbeing. It's the result of working, playing, and loving considerately, **not being a victim of your own needs.**

It's a very practical journey, starting with a renewed commitment every day, ending in contentment and appreciation - every day - however tough some of those days may be. Happiness is about treasuring the simple joys of life. It's about pursuing the good without grasping, and receiving the bad without suffering. It's a state of mind that supports you in good and bad times. It's not something that changes every time your situation changes. And there is **only one address for happiness - your own**; only one possible time to experience it - now.

In this chapter, we would like to offer you a bouquet of hints. Just a few simple inward-looking suggestions. It's no magic manifesto, yet a few thoughts which, if practised over a lifetime, one day at a time, will most definitely have a compound effect on your happiness level. Many of these practical cues may indeed even be well-known to you – and may already be well-entrenched as habits in your life. If so, use them as confirmations.

Please don't see the suggestions as a recipe to achieve instant emotional comfort. Remember, happiness is work, not magic. There is a lot of rewiring involved. Rather regard these few pages as a menu from which you may choose to gradually influence your approach to life.

It's important that you personalize and **establish the suggestions as guidelines in your day-to-day activity map**, depending on where you are in your life, being aware where you come from. We all are different and all have different perspectives. But we can all change, if we choose to and do what it takes.

> "Misery is among the most democratic of all life experiences."
>
> ANON

It's up to you...

There is nobody and nothing around to make this 'happiness' thing happen for you. Stop looking on the outside. Declare yourself accountable. And turn inward.

You have to come to the decision (if you haven't yet) that only you can be held responsible for your happiness - that only you can be blamed if you are not happy. Peace, inner fulfillment and contentment are private, 'object-lite' sensations. You shape them in the space only you can reach.

Once you have taken ownership of your happiness, it becomes a practical, manageable affair. It turns into a way instead of an event, a process instead of a means. It clears the way for a momentous shift in your spiritual maturity.

Happy people don't expect circumstances to shape their happiness. Embrace the responsibility.

Map your way…

Create the time to plan. It's as if the world is friendlier to a person with a plan.

Planning is unfortunately not an activity you can practise 'on the fly' or 'in the shower'. It's an intellectually absorbing activity and demands your full attention. Set time aside for it and work off an agenda that covers all the bases of your life. Make it a formal activity in your life. You do it in business; why should it be different in your own life?

Create a decent pause once a year for an annual review of your life. Walk away from that retreat with revived directional decisions and a set of fresh priorities for the next 12 months.

Follow through with monthly reviews. Shape every month around your priorities. End a week by allowing for an hour to fine-tune your diary for the next seven days. And every morning when you enter your day, have a clear vision of the results you want to walk away with.

Happy people concentrate their energy and optimize their time. Own up to your future.

> *"For tomorrow belongs to the people who prepare for it today."*
>
> AFRICAN PROVERB

Live in gratitude…

Imagine you lost everything. Everything you own, your loved ones, your health, your freedom…everything. Now imagine you got it all back tomorrow. How happy would you be tomorrow?

Be grateful on purpose. Learn to appreciate what you have, even the small things, all of them, every day. How can you expect more from life if you aren't even aware of what you already have?

More won't do it for you if a little doesn't do it. Spare a moment, regularly, to salute life's little miracles and nuggets, even those that aren't that pretty. Watch them, touch them, hear them, smell them, feel them, talk to them.

Treasure your blessings – write them down if you need to, every day, until you are fully aware of them. Find things to approve of instead of disapprove. Turn your common days into thanksgivings. Focus on the things that work instead of slaving away at an inventory of what you are missing. Stop whining. Laugh more. Ask less.

Life is a privilege. We are invited for a brief moment to experience its elegance. Behave like a guest to a once-in-a-lifetime event.

Happy people cherish life. Softly hold onto the opportunity to be around for a while.

Retain your zest...

Spice up your basic program regularly. Don't become a slave to a joyless schedule. Own more of your diary.

Create opportunities for new discoveries. Decommission outdated routines. Visit interesting places. Look for opportunities to grow. Seize amusing moments. Question your schedule. Learn from someone.

Happy people don't settle for energy decay. Prune your habits.

Serial time wasters in the lives of professionals

1. A priority blur
2. Interruptions and electronic 'pop-ups'
3. Meetings for the sake of meeting
4. Terminal urgencies and crises; poor planning
5. Saying yes to unimportant commitments
6. Travelling

(If these points are relevant to you, treat yourself to one suggestion next to each point with the aim to take back ten percent of the time wasted – and continue the habit)

Let it go...

Cut back on clutter. Happiness is rooted in simplicity. Modern society will present you with an assembly of excuses to live an emotionally complicated and inherently stressful life.

Lift yourself above the noise and hold onto what's really important. Free up your spirit. Walk away from nonsense. Clean the slate.

Complexity doesn't eliminate itself. It's an ultimate hoarder – inviting more of the same! You eliminate complexity by indentifying low-value glut – and throwing it off.

Know what is important when you start your days. Excuse yourself from what is not important during your days. Let go of mental garbage at the end of your days.

A happy spirit is a litter-free one. Travel light.

A hatful of tips from an old farmer

1. Life is simpler when you plough around the stump
2. Always drink upstream from the herd
3. The biggest troublemaker on your farm watches you from the mirror every morning
4. Every path has a few puddles
5. Keep skunks and bankers at a distance
6. If you get to thinking you're a person of some influence, try ordering your neighbor's dog around
7. When you wallow with pigs, expect to get dirty
8. Good judgment comes from living through many seasons, but the stickiest lessons come from bad judgment in some of those seasons

Limit your frustrations...

Trim your expectations. A disappointment is ever so often the result of loaded expectations. Aim high, set firm goals, and expend good energy on what you want to achieve, but avoid constant regret by always providing ample margin for error.

A mindset of modest expectations fuels calmness, and sees to a life filled with many positive episodes and ample pleasant surprises. It's not a question of settling for mediocrity; it's the wisdom to flow with reality.

Happy people don't over-expect. Be pragmatic.

Keep your distance…

The only person on the entire planet you have real leverage on is yourself. Although we would love to believe it, we don't hold effective domain over any people.

If you want someone else to behave differently, the only workable strategy is to adjust your own behavior. You cannot productively control, own, change, press, or motivate someone else. These are things we can only do to and for ourselves.

When you let go of forceful interference, your true influence increases. When you change your own behavior, behavior around you will change. The fewer words you use, the more people listen. The less pressure you apply, the quicker the response you hope for.

Happy people understand that the only lives they can direct are their own. Invest in your own behavior instead of trying to change someone else.

Non-forceful ways with the best chance of influencing someone's behavior

1. Share valuable information
2. Listen non-judgementally
3. Answer questions objectively
4. Change what you expect from him
5. Change the way you respond to her
6. Encourage him
7. Recognise her achievements
8. Not allowing him to become dependent on your resources, availability, and sympathy

Steer clear...

Not all information is valuable information. Jealously guard the entrance to your mind. Don't get paralyzed by every story. Carefully select what you listen to, read or believe. Own the access to your thoughts. Regard your mind as a premier facility.

Beware of buying into the dramatization of life that makes the mass media successful. They capitalize on what is called our 'negative bias' – our capacity to make more of bad news than of equivalently good news. The intellectual junk food it punts supports a thinking pattern riddled with pessimism, eventually coloring all our experiences, and skewing all our decisions. Move out of the space of toxic intentions and sensationalized information.

Happy people afford themselves a balanced, nutritious intake of information. Up your intellectual taste.

Mind the facts...

Stop using the words 'all, always, and never'. Learn to single out the moment, as 'a' moment, or the event, as 'an' event.

See one person doing it, not 'all' people. Accept that it is different this time, instead of reading that it will 'always' be like this. Intellectual oversimplification degrades our minds and leads to unproductive decisions.

Happy people don't burden their thinking with generalisations. Be specific!

> *"A sad life story is marked by unfortunate, external deficiencies. A tragic story is one in which defeat stems from the unaddressed internal flaw of poor thinking."*
>
> ANON

Quid pro quo...

You are the chief creator of the respect others afford you. People will learn how to treat you by watching how you treat yourself.

If you neglectfully harm yourself, others will probably mistreat you as well. If it is clear that you care for yourself, for your time, for your family, for your finances...you will be treated with extra courtesy.

Broken windows and chipped paint send a message that nobody is in charge and that nothing matters. A building that is in order and well-maintained commands respect. The same applies to a human life. Public respect starts at self-respect.

Happy people enjoy respect because they regard themselves. Mould your own esteem.

Leaving a footprint...

If you choose to be a parent, choose to be a loving one. Treasure your children – understand the responsibility of shaping a new life.

Fortunately, children do not expect perfection, just explicit, unconditional love. Spoil your kids with affection, laughter, and lots of time together. Accept them unreservedly. Show compassion and patience. Earn their respect. Demonstrate good values. Do it from day one.

You have one opportunity to raise your child, to sculpt another human being. Respect the extensive consequences of your effort. There is no joy as great as witnessing the success and happiness of your children later on in life, and knowing that you had something to do with it. You can never spoil children by making them too happy.

Happy parents are devoted parents. Give enough of yourself.

Parenting going wrong

1. Having an 'unwanted' child
2. Saying one thing while demonstrating another
3. Talking down
4. A disruptive relationship between parents
5. Self-absorbed; listening without hearing
6. Trying to live your life through your child
7. A stern and punitive style
8. Trying to outsource affection to a nanny or school
9. Playing your children off against each other
10. Being emotionally absent or cold
11. Being impatient and temperamental in your interactions
12. Underestimating the formative importance of the pre-school years

(If you are a parent, define the opposites of these points as guiding principles)

Modify the message...

We all have a little voice that talks to us in our heads. It articulates messages with a huge influence on our lives. It's our own voice, consistently chatting away in the corridors of our subconscious mind.

One of the biggest drawbacks of this hidden conversation is that it concentrates on explaining our deficiencies to us. It shouts out the things we get wrong. It warns us against impending failure. It reminds us of our shortcomings.

Override your inner self-talk, whenever you catch yourself participating in it, by consciously reminding yourself of the things you get right. Reinstruct your subconscious mind. Dull its effort to highlight failure by intentionally countering it with the inventory of your successes.

When you practise a different pattern of thoughts, you reinforce those neural pathways and in the process change your brain chemistry.

Happy people have a constructive inner voice. Remind yourself of what went well.

Weigh with care...

Learn to gauge the size of a disappointment with a longer-term mindset. You should always ask yourself, "How serious will this setback be five years from now?"

It's so easy to be absorbed by immediate imperfections, but so few of them are of any true significance. Most of them aren't even relevant a month from now.

Happy people maintain perspective. Learn to 'right-size' your problems.

An expensive hobby...

The demise of most empires had one thing in common – a debt burden.

Beware of debt! Buy something when you can pay for more than a third of it in cash. Live in your financial present. Debt is the consequence of trying to live tomorrow's life, today. Once that becomes a habit, your present income will never be enough.

Be realistic about what you can really afford. Don't buy through the eyes of others. Showing off is expensive. The sinking feeling after the rush of an excessive credit purchase is just not worth it.

Financiers are most helpful when you get the desire to spend tomorrow's money today, but not in explaining the compound effect this privilege has on your personal financial affairs over time. Debt is expensive! Borrowing too much money normally plunges you in playing catch-up, sometimes for the rest of your life.

Happy people are at peace with their present financial capacity. Approach credit with great care.

> *"Debt is the slavery of the free."*
> PUBLILIUS SYRUS

At your doorstep…

Many people aspire to GO TO heaven or a similar divine destination. Different religions, philosophies, and traditions all portray this magic place and the path leading there in their own unique ways.

In the meantime, very few people choose to BE there now, while still being around. They decline the experience of wonder, while still being part of this world.

Divinity on earth is a fairly quiet place. So many of us miss its entrance in pursuit of the 'one-day' version; being fixated on the 'heaven up there', the one to be received as a reward.

Heaven on earth is not a receivable, but a space of bringing joy, giving love and causing peace. It's present in the moments when you share a slice of your soul. When you show sincerity, listen with compassion, show empathy. When you choose to bring comfort and show generosity instead of being self-obsessed. When you help someone to heal instead of choosing to harm. When you act as an equal instead of posing as a superior.

Happy people craft moments of grace. Step into paradise.

Go for quality...

Most of the advice on relationships tries to guide people on 'how to make it work'. Ours is slightly different. We suggest you consider walking away from those that are not working.

Only allow real friends and constructive relationships in your life. Be selective on who you spend time on and with. Don't suffer abuse or superficial associations – you gain by avoiding it, you don't 'lose out' on a relationship. Have as little as possible interaction with cynics. Beware of self-centered people. Don't take part in conversations that are built on gloomy intent. Beware of opportunistic companionships.

A real relationship leaves both parties with more energy. It's a safe, soft place rich in trust and care. Sound friendships are not built on guilt or indebtedness, and not sustainable when marked by dependence or exploitation.

Preserve your own energy – don't let it leak through the cracks of shallow, forced or selfish relations – not socially, not in a wider family context, not in business. 'Less is more' in the world of real relationships. As wonderful as good relationships are, the consequences of accommodating the wrong people in your life can be severe.

Happy people have empowering relationships; they are not swarmed by a demanding crowd or exploitive individuals. Be exclusive.

No flipping channels...

Productive multi-tasking is a contradiction in terms. We cannot do more than one thing well at a time. It has become one of the most damaging myths out there.

If you watch a lioness hunting in the wild, she will focus on one wildebeest. She never focuses on more than one – because she knows the odds of missing both are stacked against her. The value of focus is still respected where survival is at stake.

Our brain can really only focus on one thing at a time.

Multi-tasking is known to slow people down by some fifty percent and increases the frequency of mistakes by up to fifty percent. When we try to multitask, our brain is actually switching between tasks, abandoning the one when attending to the other. It leaves your brain in a state of semi-attendance.

Our persistence in trying to get our brain to focus on more things at once has trained it to have an attention deficit. Some people simply cannot focus for any significant period of time anymore.

Sharpen up your intellect by returning to the habit of doing one thing at a time. Rediscover the value of consecutive tasking, instead of settling for the quality dilution associated with simultaneous tasking. Exceptional work is always associated with periods of deep concentration. Nothing excellent ever comes from a scattered effort.

Happy people are one place at a time. Take back the magic of concentration.

Stillness...

Harness your soul. Make ample time to practise peace. Allow yourself enough silence. Use the religion, philosophy, technique, or tradition of your preference to deepen your consciousness and harmonise your spirit.

Your inner self demands as much care and nurturing as your body does. It's the deep soil out of which you grow your life. If you cultivate your spirit and emotionally reload, the stresses of life will find it difficult to erode the serenity you carry. Resilience and renewal start from within; peace re-equips the body with its natural defences.

Happy people make ample time to nurture their souls. Seek silence.

> "It has often occurred to me that
> a seeker after truth has to be silent."
>
> GANDHI

Be exceptional...

You have to earn your living on earth, that's just the way it is. We all have to 'hunt to eat' - and the quality of your effort will determine the size of your reward. Personal financial strain often starts with conducting your career in a careless way.

Be serious about your job. Be proud of your business. Be good at what you decide to do for a living; leave successes and a positive reputation behind you. Be brilliant at one thing at a time, rather than being average at many. Concentrate your effort. Show consistency and follow through.

Never just occupy a position – be the product, the brand. When your work becomes soulless, your whole life becomes stale.

Make a hobby of your career. Show the courage to establish yourself in a field that resonates with who you are. Opt for a job that positively excites and interests you. Then build skill and become great at it. A job well done always carries a mark of passionate intensity.

Happy people enjoy what they do, or adjust their range of tasks until their job is enjoyable. Allow yourself greatness.

Use them sparingly…

Talk with care! Once it's out, it's really out there.

Words feed behavior, your own and of those around you. Every time you talk, you push a bio-chemical button and trigger certain emotions. What's more, words are interpreted by your brain as self-instructions. What you regularly say shapes your behavior – and the behavior towards you. You eventually experience the life you describe.

Mind your words when you describe life, when you depict your experiences or express an opinion. If you get into the habit of using disempowering language, your brain will simply follow the cue and diligently ensure that this pattern is embedded in all elements of your life. Talk up, express hope, describe solutions, voice kindness, articulate options, and avoid killer phrases.

Happiness is not only revealed in words, but also created by words. Weigh what you say.

Phrases of self-limitation

1. I don't measure up...
2. I should have...
3. It's her fault...
4. This is just the way I am...
5. I can't do anything about it...
6. What's the point...
7. I'm too old for...
8. I've tried that before...
9. It's too late now...
10. It's ok in theory, but...
11. They will think...
12. You can't teach an old dog new tricks...
13. Yes, but...

(Add another few 'killer phrases' you want to get rid of - and outlaw the whole list from your vocabulary)

Accept its relevance…

Make peace with your history, especially the patchy parts. We all had to go through the things we went through to get us where we are today.

Our biggest spiritual growth takes place on the back of tough times. Look back at those moments as an opportunity you have been afforded to deepen. Some might have been really dark, but take hold of them, even with help if you need it, and turn them into the necessary hurdles you had to cross along your journey.

Only when you accept and honor these events of your past, will you be able to retire them gracefully.

Happy people accept all chapters of their life story. Allow the lessons of your past to make you stronger.

Free yourself...

Learn to forgive. It is impossible to have a negative emotion in the absence of blaming someone or something. The most important element to continuous mental rinsing is to practise forgiveness. The more you do it, the easier it becomes.

The heaviest load to carry is a grudge. Holding onto hurt is a habit that buckles the spirit. If you choose to, you will always find reasons to hold onto pain, to answer unfairness with vengeance, to ponder retaliation. Clinging to bitterness harms you more than the object of your aversion. It is never the unforgiven who suffers, but the one who carries the bitterness.

Forgiveness is a soothing attitude for yourself. The act has very little to do with the culprit, or with condoning wrong behavior. It's a habit of allowing yourself a life of liberty.

Happy people refuse to entertain resentment. Let go of your own throat.

One life…

Stress is not a virus. Nor does it arrive in another human being. No external condition has the ability to create stress. The elements of life simply interact with us. What we make of these conditions is up to us. If they do result in constant stress, the problem normally sits in our own contradicting, pre-determined positions.

Stress results from living a life in your head that's not compatible with the one under your feet. You actually choose to live in conflict with reality – and then have to cope with the strains of the paradox you create.

Learn to flow with the elements of life. Obviously, some are harsh. But don't spend your everyday life in the 'opposition benches'. Stop blaming someone or something if your own mental map is flawed. Become more flexible in your approach. Have the courage to bow to the wind. Stop trying to be 'right' every time. Let go of those rigid attachments.

Happy people are in harmony with life as it is. Suspend your illusions.

> *"Our firmest convictions often mark our most important limitations."*
>
> ANON

Challenge yourself...

There is a difference between living and simply being alive. The greatest satisfaction in life comes from breaking new ground. Stretch yourself!

Personal growth is the result of tackling and overcoming difficult challenges. Engage life with energy and hang in a little longer. Persist.

Oppose the complacency that comes with order, affluence, and comfort. Refuse a 'tick-tock' life. Unlock your full potential. Find ways to reach out to new frontiers all the time. Be more. Fully explore your talent. View defeat as temporary.

If you are in the second half of your life, this message is even more relevant. Live until your last day. Continue to challenge your mind. Stay valuable. Choose to never retire from intellectual stimulation and spiritual meaning.

Happiness is about making the most of your one life. Retain your hunger to grow.

Let them be...

Mind your own business. You can never be better off by concerning yourself with analyzing someone else's life, or finding other people guilty or inferior. Stop judging people, it's energy spent in vain.

Ironically, judgmental people are the bewildered ones in the end, exhausted by the endless mental effort to strengthen themselves by weakening others. Find ways to fill your life with meaning instead of building punishing philosophies around the lives of others, or competing with those not even aware of the race. Don't build your victories upon the misfortune of others.

If you do concern yourself with someone else's life, let it be an effort to leave that person better off instead of an attempt to massage your own ego, or a push to strengthen your relative position.

Happy people aren't threatened by others. Stay in the life where you can make a real difference – your own.

Recover...

Be well rested. Sleep when and as much as you are supposed to sleep. A good night's sleep is one of a healthy body's 'secret weapons'.

Exhaustion amplifies negative stress and shortens your life. Lack of sleep reduces your gift to solve problems and leaves you with a chronic concentration deficiency. You are not brave when you suffer from sleep deprivation – you are committing prolonged suicide!

Sleep allows your brain to perform vital maintenance and gives your immune system time to mount energetic attacks against intruders you are not even aware of. Take note of the generally accepted advice that we need between seven and nine hours of sleep a night.

Happy people are rested people. Lights out.

How people deny themselves a good night's rest

1. Varying bedtimes
2. A physically passive life
3. Late or large dinners
4. A restless bedroom
5. Late-night smoking or drinking
6. Being tense before lights-out
7. Disorganised days - unfinished business
8. 'Brain work' after hours

(What can you do to improve the quality of your sleep?)

Share your soul...

Be good to people in need. Being human to each other overrides many of life's tangible setbacks. It's a fulfilling way of living.

Selflessness does not imply being irresponsible with your resources. Neither does it mean you should be a crutch to lazy opportunists, or provide for those who have given up on themselves. It's about much more than writing a check, handing out hampers, or sharing the leftovers. It's not a guilt trip. It's about giving privately and quietly of yourself, without an expectation of receiving anything in return.

The true heroes of life aren't perfect. They are simply human when it matters. They restore dignity, fuel hope, afford respect, and ignite courage. They alleviate hurt. They are angels in ordinary clothes, handing out the bounty of life from the brimful coffers of their soul.

Your happiness cannot decrease if you share it. It cannot increase if you deprive someone else of happiness. Happiness works like a candle; many can be lit from it, without shortening its life.

Happy people deflect rays of sunshine upon those in darkness, giving what currency cannot purchase.

Lighten up...

A dose of laughter is medicine to the soul. And the funniest moments are wrapped in life's small imperfections.

Lightheartedness is an attitude. Humor gives you the guts to go on when life looks its worst. Stay in touch with the funny side of life. Watch a comedy, make time for a fun read, visit a toy store, play with your child, see the irrelevance in something serious...

Never allow your laugh to become a smirk. Preserve its innocent spontaneity. Allow it to be an unpolluted source of energy.

Happy people often chuckle at life. Be cheerful.

> *"You are never fully dressed without a smile."*
>
> FROM ANNIE, THE MUSICAL

Safe hands...

Know what you do with your money. Be a true custodian of your earnings and use it thoughtfully.

If you are financially sloppy, having more money won't solve your problem; the leakage will continue. Every time you open your purse, you express your competence to cope with the responsibility that comes with stewardship.

It may sound boring, but live within a budget. See that you have one for a start. If you act within a sensible financial framework, you won't worry about every cent you spend – you will actually enjoy it. To forever fight the losing battle of living beyond your means eventually tears down your overall sense of satisfaction with life.

Money has a way of, at some point, leaving shoddy hands forever, looking for a safer haven. Wastefulness always ends in hardship.

Buy with discretion. Identify the emotional margin on a price tag. Justify value. Don't overpay. Don't overstock. Don't compete and compare. Never allow possessions to own you. Steer away from the belief that happiness is a function of purchasing power. Find something better to do than to shop when you have time on hand or a mood to beat.

Happy people work well with their money. Choose to be in charge.

What they never taught us about 'purchasing power'

1. Having three of something is not three times better than having one; the additional value of 'more' peaks sooner than you would imagine

2. Living in idyllic comfort often leads to depression; wealth-induced boredom often ends in spirit cancer

3. The value of consumer items depreciates at an astonishing speed; the emotional margin in the purchasing price quickly evaporates, and material erosion is a fact of physics

4. Our mental pleasure centre adapts very quickly to new experiences; when you are a pleasure hunter, your quest is about improving on the previous experience

5. Our assets can imprison us; many people become the janitors of their possessions

6. Someone else will always own more than you; there is no end to the journey of 'having what they have'

7. Overt affluence introduces shady newcomers to your life; wealth attracts parasites and opportunists

8. You learn most about people when they have money or when they don't have money; financial conditions shed light on who you already are

(Are your financial pursuits free of flaws and perceptions?)

Switch off the alarm...

Resist fear, in whatever shroud it visits you. Turn your back on any mental message that you 'lack'. Walk away from the inner refrain telling you that you 'fall short'. Don't entertain all the 'threats out there' in your conversations. Stop placing life in good and bad categories. Shut down the 'they win, I lose' program.

Our ancient survival brain bombards us with subconscious messages of pending harm and imminent dangers. It's an outdated fear-centre of limited value, sitting at the core of all the emotional hardship our modern society struggles with.

If you are serious about your happiness, you will gradually replace the chapters of this fear-based script with subject matter that represent abundance, self-acceptance and rational solutions.

Happy people resist their 'pain brain'. Call the bluff.

Now counts…

Unhappiness is often the result of trying to escape the present.

The present is the only real tense. Be fully where you are. This day is important. Cherish its finite nature. Time is not a dry-run.

Your future is determined by how you practically spend your days, not by how imaginative your dreams or elaborate your philosophies of life are. Having goals is important, as long as you realize that a wish-list alone does not carry you over one inch of ground. The realization of your ambitions will be determined by the quality of effort during your days.

Be friendly to your future by breaking your life up in dynamic day-long building blocks. Let every twenty-four hours count. Hold yourself to what's really important. In the end, your future will prove to be an accumulation of the content of your days.

Happy people value their days. Ensure a high-value present.

Inspection time...

Take stock, regularly. Examine your ways. Allow yourself the revitalising habit of honest introspection.

List what needs to be changed, those elements that cause more damage than good – in whatever domain of your life, however small or prominent. Include your thoughts on that list if needed. Even revisit your values and beliefs from time to time. Then construct a plan on how to address these issues – and consciously start chipping away the glut.

Don't get used to yourself! To fully live is a dynamic experience – of endlessly trimming the detail in your life, continuously eliminating habits of harm, actively building a better way, selecting more relevant options.

Happiness is not a static affair. Rethink and renew.

> *"You will never change your life until you change things you do daily."*
> MIKE MURDOCK

Access control…

We are designed to live a long life – not to die pre-maturely. What we have learned to consume however, radically alters this privilege.

You are what you eat. Food can be the most powerful preventative medicine, or in time the most influential eradicator of wellbeing. The world is obsessed with famine – yet most people die of food. We are the only species that chooses to be self-destructive eaters.

Use your discretion and all the commonly available information about a healthy, balanced diet. Fight disease in the cheapest possible way – by assisting your immune system to prevent damage in the first place. Your body is patient, inherently strong and forgiving. It doesn't demand second-to-second perfection, just consideration for what it is capable to process over a lifetime.

Mind your every-day diet. Now and then remind yourself of what your dietary habits would have been if you were busy recovering from cancer.

Include ample food known for its nutritional and restorative value; limit the health culprits. Why consciously destroy the physical head office from which you are mandated to manage your happiness? To beat health setbacks may be noble; to prevent them is wise.

Happy people live in happy bodies. Nourish yourself!

Damaging dietary habits to avoid

1. Too little daily intake of water
2. Not enough fresh fruit and vegetables
3. No regular intake of whole grain, nuts, cereals and olive oil
4. Overindulgence, followed by crash dieting
5. Too much red meat, starch, additives and refined sugar
6. Relying on supplements as magic bullets
7. Too much coffee, fizz drinks, and alcohol
8. Irregular meals: heavy dinners, no breakfasts

(How are you going to turn around the ones applicable to you?)

Tidy up...

Your mind emulates the environment it is exposed to. Accordingly, your bottom drawer mirrors the degree of order in your head.

Organize your intimate space. A tidy personal setting rubs off on your mind. Clean up the mess. File what should be filed, fix what is broken, paint what should be painted, and throw out what has reached its sell-by date.

Look at your environment as a photograph of your mind. Afford yourself orderliness, even where no-one can see.

Happiness looks for a neat head. Help it to be - with a shipshape environment.

> *"You don't get in life what you want; you get in life what you are."*
> — LES BROWN

First ones first...

A functional pattern of relationships has an 'inside-out' character to it.

It starts right in the middle – establishing and harnessing a caring relationship with yourself. If you cannot be a good friend to yourself, you are deprived of fundamental relationship capacity before you even enter the wider world of people. Are you a truthful friend to yourself?

Once you have a solid relationship with yourself, your focus should preferably move to those sharing your intimate space with you – the individuals in your household. They are very important people in your relationship grid – way more than any 'stranger' out there. Are you a valued and respected partner, mentor, and friend in your own home?

If you ensure that you are solid relationship material 'at the centre', you are equipped to be a valued member in a constructive, wider social context as well. Your professional associates, historic acquaintances, extended family, and social companions will have a quality person to relate to.

Happy people craft loving relationships in their immediate circle first. Charity starts at home!

> *"Tell me what company thou keepst, and I'll tell thee what thou art."*
>
> — MIGUEL DE CERVANTES

Observantly there...

Engage life thoughtfully. Be one with it.

Learn to embrace every moment as a hand-crafted present. Slow down to allow the marvels of life to present themselves.

Look at the stars as if they only appear every hundred years. Hold your loved ones as if it's your last day together. Eat a peach as if it's a personal gift from a God. Make a garden as if you expect a visit from a king. Look at rain as if it brings the end to famine.

Happy people magnify life's snippets of loveliness. Celebrate the ordinary.

Shut the door...

You don't always have to be with people. Constant availability is not a good idea. Excusing yourself is ok.

Your most important insights emerge when you afford yourself reflective space. Your best work awaits you in private silence. Your biggest breakthroughs emerge after extended periods of uninterrupted concentration. Your sense of calmness is rooted in your ability to socially detach on a regular basis.

Happy people value stillness. Afford yourself the sanctity of privacy.

> *"All men's miseries derive from not being able to sit in a quiet room alone."*
> BLAISE PASCAL

Be active…

A car corrodes if you don't use it. A human body has certain 'mechanical' realities to it as well.

Inject your body with energy and afford it the cleansing it needs – exercise enough! Our bodies are designed for activity but our clever brains have designed a world of passivity. Evolution has shaped us to enjoy idleness – and we still pursue it. Our health suffers largely as a result.

Regular physical activity supports an upward spiral of feeling good and for many people creates a more positive health outlook over time. It helps you to relax, enhances energy levels and has numerous health benefits.

Get professional advice about the relevant physical workout you should follow – and answer your body's call for purification and an energy refill.

Happiness is about active self-preservation. Get moving.

Preventing rainy days…

Overlooking the financial realities of retirement dents many people's quality of life in their senior years. Approach your retirement with open eyes. Financial independence is the end result of a very logical lifetime practice.

Guard over your nest egg. Understand that you may live longer than was the case with previous generations. This means that you will need more financial resources to finance the post-retirement phase of your life than you may realise. Provide for it while you have the opportunity.

Financial peace of mind after a lifetime of work keeps you young and energised. Make it easy on yourself – save first, then spend, whatever your income. Saving is a habit, not a function of income. Know the savings number that will make retirement possible for you. The earlier you make 'saving-a-percent-of-income' part of your financial agenda, the less radical the lifetime challenge.

If possible, never stop earning an income while you are healthy, whatever your age. And when you do decide to retire, accept the income-providing capacity of your pool of assets. Calculate the lifestyle your assets can finance, with professional assistance, don't guess it. Then live within the long-term means your life savings allow.

Happy people don't set themselves up for hardship. Take charge of your financial destiny.

The profile of financially independent people

1. A lifetime habit of 'underspending'; they saved at least fifteen percent of their gross income during their working life
2. Didn't fake work or scatter their effort; they looked after their careers and deepened their skill
3. As a rule seldom 'overpaid' for assets or consumer items; they were value conscious
4. Were generally lifestyle-debt averse; they repaid their debt sooner than they were allowed to
5. Not inclined to make 'sweeping' lifestyle changes; they were less impulsive
6. Chipped away at it; they weren't 'lucky', did not pursue excessive investment returns, and walked away from exotic financial solutions
7. Maintained their existing assets; they had more because they cared for what they already had
8. Fewer crises and recoveries; they looked after their overall wellness
9. More private; they didn't live through the eyes of others
10. More content; they didn't try to fix the past, turbo the future, or set others straight
11. Weren't married to their business ownership; they diversified their investments away from one company at some point

(Is your style financially-independent friendly?)

Patient yet persistent...

We are not designed to make revolutionary shifts in life. The discomfort of sweeping changes to your pattern of living holds the danger of early defeat. We have been shaped by a history of gradual progression. To change therefore takes time.

Any radical insight you may take from this book will be of optimal value to you if you back it with evolutionary implementation. A drastic long-term shift in your capacity to be happy depends on the small daily changes you are willing to make. Training is at the core of any improvement in a skill.

This basic truth is applicable to all areas of your life; happiness as well. You will achieve most through establishing new routines in support of any new principle you introduce to your life. There is nothing romantic about ambitious failures.

Repetition is the key activity of any form of fitness. Incremental advances, constantly pursued, become permanent qualities. You conquer a summit by chipping away at the mountain trail.

Happiness is not the result of erratic change. Back your intent with small, conscious shifts in your daily conduct.

Making up our minds

A 92-year-old, petite, proud lady was fully dressed that morning by eight o'clock. Her hair was fashionably coifed and make-up perfectly applied. She was moving to a nursing home that day.

After a long wait in the lobby of the nursing home, she smiled sweetly when told her room was ready. As she maneuvered her walker to the elevator, she was provided a visual description of her tiny room, including the eyelet sheets that had been hung on her window.

"I love it", she stated with the enthusiasm of an eight-year-old who had just been presented with a new puppy.

"Mrs Jones, you haven't seen the room yet, please just wait."

"That doesn't have anything to do with it!", she replied. Happiness is something you decide on ahead of time. "Whether I like my room or not doesn't depend on how the furniture is arranged... it's how I arrange my mind. I have already decided to love it. It's a decision I make about my life every morning when I wake up."

CHAPTER 5

A FEW LAST WORDS

THIS BOOK WAS NOT MEANT to be a scientific masterpiece nor an empirical research document. It had a simple aim – to draw your attention to the dynamics of personal happiness. There is so much more to say, but we are going to leave it at this.

We want to end with a personal note of encouragement.

We would like to invite you to take full responsibility to further your own level of happiness. We appeal to you to pursue a fulfilling life – don't wait for it to happen. You are worthy of happiness, but need to actively reach out for it.

Wherever you go from here, whatever you decide to do with your life, live in love. Allow this everlasting wellspring of happiness in your life. Real love is not a feeling; it is giving without remembering and receiving without forgetting. It is not something to search for; it is something to hand out. There is no satisfaction greater than being loving. No fear can ever stand before the power of unqualified compassion. Release the conditions you place on your love. To truly care is the only door to heaven on earth.

Learn from pain, don't succumb to it. Then move on. We cannot always enjoy dominion over everything. There is no perfection out there, so expect distress and setbacks from time to time. If you are willing to learn from hurtful events, you prevent more of them from happening to you.

Don't take life personally. And remember, no one owes you.

Talk with care. Besides other people taking cues from your words, your mind listens to your commands and your spirit takes on the sentiment you express.

Show courage. Make decisions. Use this wonderful human ability to not be a victim. Choose to be better off. The more you opt to move forward, the stronger your sense of freedom will become, because people who act gain personal liberty.

Define who you are – start now – and be the best of that person you can be, every day. Happiness is a present state. Don't wait for the future or other people to come to your rescue. Work around your weaknesses, optimise your strengths. Create your own reality.

Regard yourself. Enjoy your own company. Look after your body. Harness your spirit. Grow your competence. Guard over your resources. Act your age.

Happiness is the art of prevention. Say no when you should.

Be a truthful friend. Start in your own home. Keep your word. Never blame, not even yourself.

Keep a healthy perspective on life. Steer away from any radical viewpoints. Learn to afford a problem its rightful size, not more. Look for opportunities. Don't get stuck. Laugh more than you cry, much more.

Make sure you know why you live. Only you can have that answer. Start every day with purpose. Live every day as if it is your last, because one day it will be.

You are the best person to determine your own destiny. If you choose happiness and embrace some of the simple attitudes and actions mentioned in this book, and consistently improve on them, happiness will find it difficult to pass you by.

Remember, you don't have to be happy for the rest of your life, only now. Be.

ABOUT THE AUTHORS

LOUIS FOURIE AND KEVIN HORSLEY are two friends who share a keen interest in the dynamics of 'the optimal life'. They come from different professional backgrounds, yet are united in their sense of optimism, love of simplicity, and belief in humans' capacity to improve.

Louis spent the first 10 years of his professional career practising as an economist in the South African financial industry and was one of the first winners of South Africa's Economist of the Year award.

He later became one of the founders of a leading South African wealth management business and acted as chairman of the group for twelve years. After retiring from corporate life, he founded The Logic Filter, a small consultancy through which he mentors young professionals and acts as an independent advisor to emerging business leaders.

Louis contributed to numerous national economic publications over the years, and co-authored a number of books on different subjects.

Kevin is a lifelong student in the field of neuroscience. He has been analyzing the mind and memory and its capacity for brilliance since

1990, looking for new and better ways to 'run your own brain' and optimize its capacity.

He is one of only a few people in the world to have received the title 'International Grandmaster of Memory'. He is a World Memory Championship medalist, and a two-time World Record holder for 'The Everest of Memory Tests'. He is an international speaker, trainer, and consultant and assists organizations in improving their thinking, motivation, creativity and learning.

A FEW WORDS OF RECOGNITION

A BOOK ON ANY SUBJECT starts off as an internal dialogue. It is the end-result of many influences, discussions, observations, and lots of research. It is the product of condensing a thousand views into a hundred words, or expanding one thought into a thousand new words - of trying to understand life a little bit better.

The written word is a blend of one's personal views and thought processes. Any book is coloured by subjectivity. But, that is the wonder of life – sharing our opinions, taking pleasure in our discoveries and thinking with each other – and so, hopefully leaving each other slightly better off.

Many great minds have been applied over time to the subject of happiness and many respected people have written about it. We would like to recognise the influence of these people's work on this book. We are talking about people such as Ruut Veenhoven, Edward Deener, Sonja Lyubomirsky, Daniel Kahneman, Dan Baker, Cameron Stauth, David Lykken, Dylan Evans, Robert Cooper, Ayman Sawaf, Peter Herschbach, Dacher Keltner, Ben van Biljon, Mark Kahn, James

O' Toole, Martin Seligman, David Hawkins, Hans Falkena, Richard Layard, Julie Norem, Dresdner Kleinwort Wasserstein Research team, William Sheldon, Athur Brooks, Desmond Morris, Wayne Dyer, Anthony Robbins, Tony Buzan, Stephen Covey, Brian Tracy, Michael Hall, Richard Bandler, Herman Hesse, Jim Rohn, Eloise Cooper, Marius Welgemoed, Lesley Garner, Anton Drotsky, Jack Canfield, Daniel Gilbert, Jonathan Haidt, Art Berg, Napoleon Hill, Terry Burnham and Jay Phelan.

Also, thank you to those we did not mention here, but who in some way said, shared or demonstrated something that enriched the message in this book.

Finally, to Niel Fourie, who was responsible for managing the technical composition of the book and bringing together the final product, a great thank you. Your contribution was outstanding.

Louis and Kevin

OTHER BOOKS BY THE AUTHORS

Unlimited Memory: How to Use Advanced Learning Strategies to Learn Faster, Remember More and be More Productive

Remembering the Presidents of the USA: The Super Quick and Easy Way to Remember all 44 Presidents of the United States

GET BOOK DISCOUNTS & DEALS

Get discounts and special deals on our bestselling books at

www.tckpublishing.com/bookdeals

ONE LAST THING...

IF YOU ENJOYED THIS BOOK or found it useful we would be very grateful if you'd post a short review on Amazon. Your support really does make a difference and we read all the reviews personally so we can get your feedback and make this book even better.

Thanks again for your support!

THE HAPPY MIND

www.ingramcontent.com/pod-product-compliance
Lightning Source LLC
Chambersburg PA
CBHW070114080526
44586CB00013B/1292